Pink & Blue

I HAD MORE TO SAY

Editing & Layout: Writer Services, LLC
Cover Design: Writer Services, LLC

ISBN 13: 978-1-942389-25-5

Prominent Books

Prominent Books and the Prominent Books Logo are Trademarks of Prominent Books, LLC

Pink & Blue

I HAD MORE TO SAY

MIKE VARGA

To Yvonne

Thank you for more than 40 years of love,
Support and partnership in growing a family,
A business, and even an adventure into poetry!

Contents

Foreword

This book is a compilation of poems written over about a 12-month period. Mostly, I wrote about whatever moved me in that moment and time. Ideas come from the news, from events, the interaction with friends and family and observations on essays or articles I've read. There's seldom any rhyme or reason to what is next. However, I've observed that this is true with most people as well. Life is chaotic. Life and events that move us are often not foreseeable. Life just happens. I hope you find some insights and some thoughts that move you as you read this collection. In this collection, there is something of an epic poem that's called Creative Worshiping. It came about partly as a challenge from a friend that suggested I should write something that was broad and sweeping and inspiring. I don't expect it to be a hit with most readers, but I hope that it does remind us that creativity is something that is uniquely a human endeavor. And that creativity is a form of worshiping our creator through the gifting of our unique value and talents to humanity. My challenge to myself is to continue to always find a way to create and to be as amazed as a child is at the wonders of the world and the creativity of others.

I wrote content over a year's time with the intent that I would compile and edit later. I found editing later as challenging as I did with my first book, but I had some great help this time.

Thank you, to my brother Dave, who volunteered to edit the first draft of this book. He found so very many errors and made some suggestions on improvements that were very helpful. Also, thank you to Robert Nahas and his team at Writer Services, LLC for their fine efforts to shape this into a book that I hope will look good on readers' nightstands or coffee tables.

Also, thank you to all of you that provide encouragement to me to keep writing. I'm forever grateful for your support!

A

Pink and Blue

I Had More to Say

This is my second book of poetry. Far from my first attempt, *That Other Side of My Brain*, which included much about my philosophy, this is just what I had to say at the moment… and I always seem to have more to say, especially about what I believe unites us as we journey through life together. I have a few discussions sprinkled in, essentially messages that I felt I needed to say at the time. For example, you'll find one on "Fixing the Church," which is paired with a poem, "Gilded Evil."

The main title of this book is taken from a poem I wrote and paired with my granddaughter's artwork. The painting is shown on the cover of this book. I know I'm biased, but I really found her composition inventive and her talent extraordinary. She called the painting *My Shoes*. But it spoke to me more simply about how we may each be different and of different hues, but we all have a role to play and purpose. Something that should make us proud—something which we can rally around as friends. A simple message, a simple poem, a beautiful piece of art.

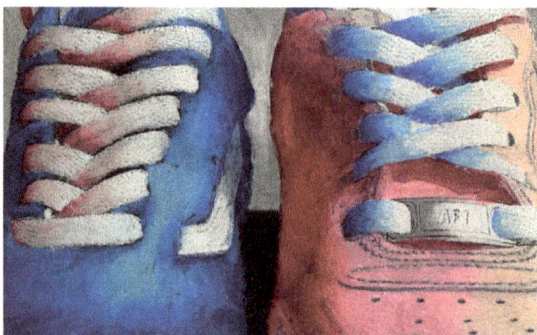

Pink and Blue

Just shoes, pink and blue
Side by side, different
But same as me and you

Where on the scale are you?
Do we disagree, maybe?
But friends no matter the hue

We serve a purpose proud
So, we acclaim ourselves
As tennis shoes out loud!

No matter pink or blue
United we're here
Always supporting you!

Left and Right

Right

Hold on to what is right
The wisdom of our forefathers
Freedom to be prosperous and safe
Liberty from oppression of others
The system is the protector of Liberty
Rule of law is the system that makes us great
People have to protect and defend their rights
To the pursuit of life, liberty and happiness
As defined by our forefathers and I as an individual
Ensuring all have equal opportunity
And overcoming past injustices with present equality
Enabling the marriage of personal responsibility
And opportunity
We've earned opportunity for wealth, health and security
And we should invest in opportunity enablement
We hold on to our right pole
But we reach to each other to be stronger as one
And

Left

Sing praise for what is right
The social conscience of humankind
Freedom to be safely who we really are
Liberty from oppression of the system
The people are the measure of the system
The rule of law changes to serve the needs of the people
People should be protected, and their rights defended
By the government of the people and for the people
And choice of what life, liberty and happiness is for me
Ensuring all human kind is treated equally
And past injustices are corrected, in our time and place
Through the marriage of our collective responsibility
And opportunity
We are owed a human wage, health and security
And we should invest in achievement of social justice
We hold on to our left pole
But we reach to each other to be stronger as one
And

Together as One   We are Stronger

Memorial Day, 2019. I watch the beauty of the American flag flying off the porch early in the morning, when the street is quiet, as neighbors sleep-in, enjoying a day off from work, and think of playing with the grandchildren today, of what I'll grill later, and then it occurs to me that the flag flies free on this porch because of the ultimate sacrifice of so many men and women who gave themselves to the fight—who gave themselves to a cause greater than any one of us. The cause of freedom, the cause of security and safety at night. It is right for us to remember them and ensure their sacrifice is memorialized in our hearts.

Memorial Day Prayer

Flag flies bright from the porch
For those who carried the torch
Into the darkness, into the awful fight
For us to enjoy freedom and safety at night
The sacrifice, of those women and men
Who answered the call, with how and when
Not why me, not find someone else to send
And they gave all they had until the very end
It is right then, that we remember and pray
For those with the angels we memorialize today

First Book Thrill

My first book was *That Other Side of My Brain*. I was quite stoked about getting it printed, and I felt it would be a perfect coffee table book—one you could pick up and read with a glass of wine or a cup of coffee. Then, one day, I went to use the bathroom at Mom and Dad's. There was my book in the basket by the toilet. Oh well, so much for the "first book thrill" and how I had envisioned it being a centerpiece of everyone's coffee table. So if you want to put this book next to the toilet for a wonderful bathroom read, then go right ahead. I'm prepared for it … but I'm going to persist in envisioning something more like this:

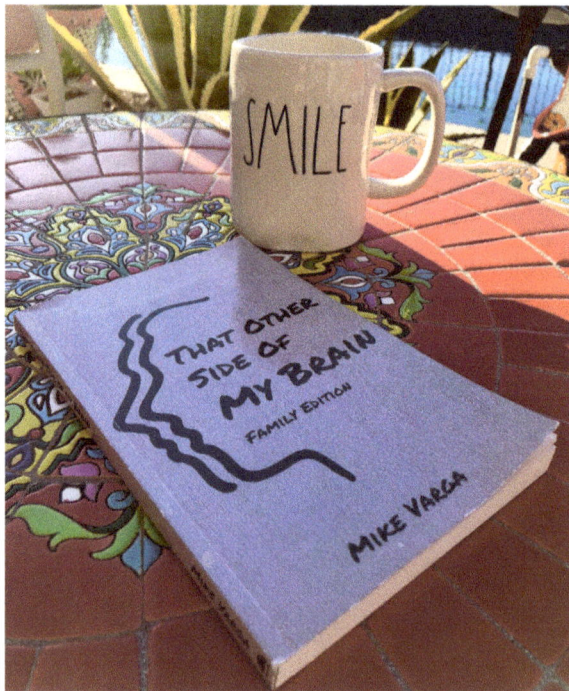

Poet's Passion

I need to write
There's something more to say
But there are things I should do
Wrapping poems into a book
But composing is passion
Sometimes I just have to write
Sometimes I have no clue what to write
Sometimes I wonder does anyone care what I write

Art inspires life and poetry
I'd like my poetry to inspire art
See the colors in my mind
Roll the words in my mouth
Taste them, feel their texture

Tell me of the children,
Not what they are doing
Or their many accomplishments
But what are they thinking and feeling
And the development of their character

The mind is important cargo
In a body nourishing and protecting
Find joy in a breeze when it's hot
A chill when there should be none
The joy of clouds when it should be clear
Even the tears of rain that streak windows
Is a state of mind?

Could I love more
Should I know how?
The cup seems full,
Yet add a few more drops if you will
I'll keep sipping from that cup every day
Feeding strength, joy and inspiration

TWEET

Tweet Storms in the Forecast…

You can probably guess where this comes from if you have been digitally aware during Mr. Trump's reign.

Flurries

Flurries of the fantastical claims
To disturb, disrupt are their aims

We are smart and can detect certain lies
But we listen and something inside us dies

Open your eyes and see the world anew
Find the truth if you can, in his word stew

And yet it continues, wind and rain
Distorting the view through the pane

Maybe we'll learn and understand
Fantasy and truth intertwine again

Pablo Picasso, self-portraits over time, from Modern Met: https://mymodernmet.com/pablo-picasso-self-portraits/

Picasso once said, "Art is a lie that reveals the truth."

Are we not the same? Do we hide behind our pride and vanity to avoid risking the truth? Our frailties, ego, and fears of failure keep us from being open about our love and being really the best we can be.

The Best We Can Be

We are truth wrapped in a lie
Our ego, our fears and silly pride

Our mothers know and can see
They know the best we can be

They've held us from moment of birth
They know all of heaven and earth

Be thankful for chance to see
The very best we all can be

Philippe Park

There's a park with ancient trees that seem to reek of history and yet they speak peacefully and beautifully near Tampa Bay. Safety Harbor is named so, because it was a place for ships to hide from the wrath of great storms.

Philippe Park was named for one of the earliest settlers, Odette Philippe. His grave marker located in the park is inscribed with his story:

Odet Philippe

Born Lyon, France, 1787
Died at this Site 1869
As the first European
settler in Pinellas County,
he established St. Helena
Plantation, now Philippe Park.
Philippe was the first
to cultivate grapefruit
in Florida and introduced
cigar-making to Tampa.
His descendants populated
this frontier. He was
said to be a doctor
and of noble birth.

Courtesy of Wikipedia

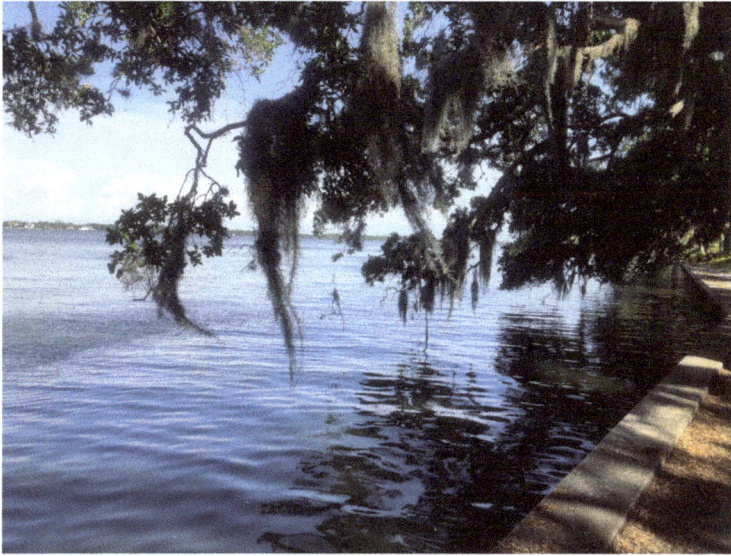

Early settlers certainly wondered at the remarkable views, ancient trees and calm waters. Fortunately, this modern community values it's parks, history and small town beauty. Worth the visit if you should find yourself in the Tampa/St. Petersburg area of Florida.

A Moment in the Park

A walk along the sparkling bay
Rest beside a two-century oak
Sit on the bench for a short stay

Granddaddy of a tree
What have you seen?
Indians, boaters, lovers, me?

What have you endured?
Scars from storms, bears?
And still shade you ensured

What memories will we have?
What of this very moment?
Will you remember and save?

I remember, and ever save

If it's Sunday morning, I'm certainly making pancakes and being thankful for the invention of boxed pancakes … a shout out here to Hungry Jack Buttermilk mix!

Pancakes

I cannot make much
But I'll make you pancakes
Buttermilk, berries and such

Chicago World's fair, 1892
Was when pancake mix in a box was introduced
Just so I can make them for you

For the kids too
Mickey Mouse is easy
A head and ears two

It's a small thing I know
But for all you do for me
It's a small thanks to show

Those clothes in the back of the closet finally fit again … too bad I'm not allowed to wear them anymore … Styles change after all.

Fat Clothes

I've got skinny clothes
I've got fat clothes

Too bad between weight events
Fashion inconsiderately changes

I've got in-fashion clothes
I've got out-of-fashion clothes

Maybe I should just wear what I like
And stop caring about changes

This one's obvious … unless you are a salesperson yourself…
or if you are one, do you allow it to happen to you too?

Salesman

Oh no what will you talk me into?
What is it that you think I should do?

With your smile, smooth voice and shine
What will you tell me I need this time?

You've got just a moment to make your play
Then I'm going to send you on your way

Oh yeah, so what does it cost again?
I don't need it, but still I'm sucked in
Geez…

The Two Hearts of Mine

The heart I live with, ensures life and health as I grow old
The heart I love with, is ever young, passionate and bold

These two hearts play on this scarred battleground landscape
Locked together and intertwined so neither can escape

They define who I am, these two beating hearts of mine
They battle for the essence of soul and eternal mind

Neither may ever truly win
As they go around and around again

That first dance, who's following who?

Follow Me Following You

Let me lead in this loving dance
Follow me in tempting romance

Or am I following you my dear
As you pull me breathlessly so near

Round and round where did we begin
There's no end as we go around again

The music I cannot hear, only feel
Faithfully following your sex appeal

Follow me, following you
Heart's music must be true

Value this life; it is short in the context of infinity of all time, and yet it is our precious eternity … and so you determine if your essence is one of love, joy and passion because you overcome the challenges of life's pain and suffering. Never allow evil and absence of God's love to be your eternity.

Eternity

It's a long time
Or a short rhyme
It's a blink of an eye
Or maybe God's sigh
For mortals such as you and me
This life's our blessed eternity

∞

Infinity

It is forever and the set of everything
Equally, it exists as infinitesimal divisions
Of time between one and nothing

∞

How many times do the same dreams repeat? We seek to find a complete and happy ending, but maybe we are just doomed to keep chasing the same dream around the clouds, never resolving, always contending … I guess if they were resolved, maybe they wouldn't be repeating dreams.…

Repeating Dreams

Dreams often do repeat
Seeming never to miss a beat

Coming around again and again
Searching for a way to win

They argue and plead
And never quite succeed

In defining truth or lie
Inexplicitly they still try

So try to find meaning
In images we are seeing

Finding our way to a happy end
Or forever repeat and contend

Dreams

Sleep at times may elude
But never allow dreams to

When you have nothing else to do, close your eyes and really think about what you see. What do your eyes tell you? What memories come to you in those waking moments with eyes closed? You may just see more than you ever thought possible. Or read these poems and see something deeper than just the words and pleasant rhymes.

Seeing With Eyes Closed

I close my eyes just to see what I'll see
Random or real, or ghosts around me

Does light find a way through lids so thin
Does blood, veins impart patterns within

I breathe easier, soothing, at rest
Eyes closed is when I see the best

Maybe it's practice that makes it right
But I see with eyes closed each day and night

And I come to know comfort herein
Eyes closed to see and remember again

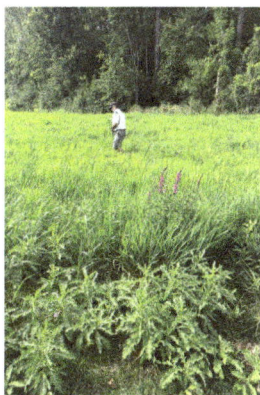

I advise staying out of the cabbage patch....

When the Ground Gives Way

Pops hit his ball badly
… into the cabbage patch and sighed
I saw it all happen
… so I went in, confident I had it eyed
But it's not so easy
… the vegetation hiding all
So, a bit of searching
… then I find that errant ball
Next, I find no ground
… after just a step on my way out
In a flash I'm on my side
… certain I'll be broken, I give a shout
Then I realize, I'm OK
… just embarrassed I had shouted "aye"
But, geez it's scary to fall
… when the ground gives way!

Fun to watch a three-year-old negotiating time to play in long summer days … His mother said to him one summer day, "The Sun forgot to go down, but you still have to go to bed!"

The Sun Forgot to Go Down

It's summer for little boys
The sun forgot to go down
So, let us play with our toys

The fireflies not glowing yet
The birds are still singing
There's another boy we just met

Down the grassy hill we run
Kicking a ball swinging a stick
It doesn't matter we're having fun

Can we play while the sun still sees!
Summer sun forgot to go down
We're having fun, so, mommy please!

A three-year-old has an amazing imagination and is never inhibited by the impossible. If we could all enjoy the wonder and imagination of when we were three.

Food Fight With Wes

He says hi, pancake pup
Hi there, hamburger boy
Do you want syrup in dipping cup
Would you like happy meal toy

Would you like berries sweet
Or ketchup and Frenchy fries
At the table lettuce meet
And mustard corn flies

Mickey Mouse pancake
Giggles at dinner or breakfast
Give it a spin and a shake
Just make food fun at last!

Today, I'm chilling in an airport lounge waiting for what seems like an impossibly long time for a flight home. Watching people come and go, finding ways to kill time themselves. I'm listening to music. I don't want to hear other conversations; it's more interesting to see and make up stories about what they are doing or talking about... it's like creating your own mysteries.

Chilling in the Airport

Is he a businessman on a sales trip
Is she a spy who just give a tail the slip

Are they running to make the last flight
If they don't make it, it'll be a long night

There are no newspapers being read
She talks and holds a phone to her head

Across from me she talks to him emphatic
He listens and holds his head dramatic

World problems solved while killing time
Mysteries and just a silly little rhyme

This iconic photo was used to illustrate separation of parents and children. However, in this specific incident, the mother and child were not separated. There are plenty of other cases where separation of families did occur.

Immigration Failure.
So many will pay for demonstrated intolerance of basic human needs and care for families. Separating children from parents must have lasting impact on lives interrupted and changed. This picture was widely published, one of many anguish-inducing scenes.

Zero Tolerance

Zero Tolerance is the demand
Heroic demonstrative, enforcement
Divide them, force them from our land

In vacuum of righteous think
Regardless the cost or loss
Compassion was the missing link

Righteous, law demanded thought
Meets the searing cry of children
Hearts turned, alternatives sought

How to undo, horrors we wrought
The terrible mess we've made
Reconnecting was never a thought

In the moment of action taken
Satisfied, to force an issue
In zero tolerance, our soul forsaken

The children will continue to cry
For years until they stop
Broken lives we must not deny

Yes, zero tolerance, was our call
Incentive to stay away
Incentive to negotiate for a wall

What will we get?
A generation failed
Our soul's regret

I have a belief that the creative process is the closest we can get to being godlike. When we use our talents to improve our understanding of science, to deliver technology, to unravel the mysteries of mathematics, to bring new ideas to life, and to create beauty in art, we are being uniquely human by helping mankind and, in such a form, worshiping the great Creator....

Creative Worshiping

Did not ancient creators value enterprise
As they invent and apply the wheel and realize
How they had reduced work as had the lever
Did humanity recognize those who were clever
Did we thank them for extraordinary contribution
As the wheel of work turned another revolution
Was Whitney valued later for the cotton gin
Did we multiply work output over and over again
Bosch and Haber found nitrogen from air they could mine
And Borlaug in praise gave us wheat hybrids to stop famine

Do we appreciate the value of light in hours of night
Was Edison worshiping when his experiment showed us light
Do we know that Tesla ensured transmission to the home
Electricity, so with a flip of finger, wondrous light is shone
Was it Marconi's worship or his electromagnetic thought
Of wondrous voices of our loved ones he brought
For Bell, whose invention allowed us to hear
Our loved ones as if they were ever so near
Did Schottky and chorus of others make transistor small
So we can carry in our pocket friends and family all
Are theories of Shannon a form of worship applied
Such information we can decipher, for which we relied

--- Health ---

Wondrous creations with no thought of wealth
Scientist with discoveries to enhance our health
Salk and others exceeded the result of an iron lung
Nobel Prizes are a way their praises can be sung
And evil dragons of heart disease can be slayed
By Ersek patented stent, properly played

Or how about the ancients who found pain relieved
Surely, they felt it important and they must've believed
That chemistry was worship of sort indeed
Born of alchemy and experiment, creativity's seed
And what of today's medical research investment
Is it wealth, or is creative worship the enticement
We should never accept that medicine is good enough
Encourage our youth to be creative and be of the right stuff

--- Physics ---

Did math and physics always exist awaiting discover
Was it creative to find great mysteries under cover
Did Newton worship the beautiful necessity of gravity
Did Einstein praise time and unbound it through relativity
Would we know of a universe and our place
Without Galileo describing Earth correctly in space
What of atoms as the nature of matter, small units, individual and distinct
Ancient philosophers describing the nature with thought and instinct
Dalton would use to define why elements react in ratios of numbers whole
Would Thompson have discovered electrons and their wondrous role
Would Bohr and so many who helped find order in the universe of small
Corollaries fascinate between the grand universality of space, atoms and all

--- Artistic ---

So too creativity of words, imagery, thought should be defined
As worship of the human soul, granted by God, but continually refined
Artistry brings out understanding, and thereby wisdom and emotion
Da Vinci worked relentlessly on a smile, which was nothing short of devotion

Did Shakespeare merely entertain, or was he saying we should examine our souls
Was Hemingway also challenging our understanding in For Whom the Bell Tolls
Did Dali bring us images that look deeper into our conscience collective
As music, rhythms and lyrics and melodies explore our world objective
Doesn't Dylan and Taylor create music and lyrics to inspire
Is not music part of God's expectation for a joyous choir
Did He not plan for us to laugh with mirth
So creative comedy must too, have great worth

--- In Our Own Way ---

Creativity is like finding your way through a thick and dense mist
Dedication, insight, perseverance and yet fog continues to resist
Appreciating the work of so many who came before
They found a way through the mist and to discovery's door
They build on each other's success, creations and insight
Creatively worshiping is humankind's God-given right

We have the right and honor to be creative in our own way
And we can give honor to creativity being inventive everyday
Decorating a room to give all who see it some beauty and delight
Find a way to curiosity, or simply showing a child wrong from right

In ways that are creative and induces life-long learning
That creative spark that sets others toward discovery yearning
Whether we paint, write, discover, or creatively repair
Using our talents to create is as human as breathing air

We appreciate the grand creations of communication, transportation, light at night
We appreciate medical understanding and practice, math, and physics brought to light
And we appreciate the opportunity to enjoy music and the beauty of art and rhyme
As the wheel of creative work, production and progress affords us that worshiping time

The world has known throughout history mostly autocratic governments. Democracy is still fighting for survival in many parts of the world. The rise of nationalism and strong autocratic rule should be concerning. Sometimes it feels that our democracy is also under threat. Will we learn from fascism's history, or are we doomed to see history repeated?

Avoid the Raging Storm

First, he sells conspiracies untrue
Blame them for what is ailing you
More loudly he entrains
Hate, mistrust all the same
We will be great again
It is us versus them
Fear and fervor, call them names
Create enemies, make false claims
Wave of discontent, a rise to power
All the others will be made to cower
Fight the truth with louder lies
Discredit the press and their allies
Take over courts, they must serve us
The nation, the people in him will trust
His will is the nation's, and their ruin
Soon this ego, this bluster is all our undoing
And the war will end, millions and he too will die
And yet his hate lives on, and still his flag will fly
So, we let another, and another, and more will try

And they come to us with their own special lie
But the story is always audacious and the same
It's untrue, but they give the enemy an ugly name
Our belief of innate superiority fans flames of the fire
The system failed us, and a faux hero is our heart's desire
We must learn from history of fascism's form
And avoid the next coming raging storm

Memory Clouds

Memory clouds give shape to a vast sky
Those fluffy thoughts in our mind's eye

Darkening storm clouds please abate
Just blow away with memories we hate

Rather great memories, bring joy of past to sunset's glow
Harboring thoughts of all the love we know

Giving way to starry skies clarity at night
As memories of life collect in a billion points of light

Our world spins faster with more time behind
Than which lies ahead, clouding memory and mind

Blessed to look at clouds from both sides in our time
Still they fascinate and memories' illusions come to rhyme

And tomorrow's clouds of anticipation do reappear
Each morning as sunrise of present is near

A new day of opportunity for friends to know
A new set of colorful memories to bestow

Thinking of the future. If we consider, we may have another million years to develop. What will we become? What of us will remain? I think the uniquely human traits that separate us from other species is our appreciation for beauty and our ability to laugh at the ridiculous and the ironic. Certainly what we believe is beautiful may change, and maybe our sense of what is funny will be more complex, but I have faith that beauty, humor and love will still matter.

A Million Years

In a million years' time, what of us will be sustained
Will we be wiser, calmer, or maybe devolved, even untamed

Will we think of our species as human or another name
Will we give voice to thoughts, will numbers be the same

I think there's hope for a higher form of mind and discourse
But laughter must survive, a sense of beauty and love, of course

Eagle Flight

Majestic eagle flying north at sunrise
Glint of white tail and head as she flies

The sun warming her right wing
Every bright morning the same thing

To her hunting grounds she goes
Why there, how is it that she knows

Is it from mothers to daughters they learn
But then which intellect was first to discern

Was a discovery of accident or intent
And a message through generations sent

As with all things, beginnings must have a start
The eagle flies majestic bringing thrill to the heart

Mile Seven

We climb through ever thinning sky
Millions of us, each day we fly

Now approaching mile seven
Just that much closer to heaven

Imagining clouds as memories below
Horizon purple with sun's dying glow

Chasing sunset into the west
Close my eyes and try to rest

And loving thoughts to be shared
Prayers certainly now to be heard

Like a million others closer to heaven
As we're leveling off at mile seven

Roundness

Someone asked if I was trying to get in shape
I said I'm in shape, it just happens to be round
Round is a shape you can rely on
It's a shape that is infinitely symmetrical
And remarkably efficient
No matter what you try to do with round
It remains persistently round
I've started running after many years
Of letting these knees recover
At least that's what I told myself I was doing
Run, well, my slo-mo version is best called jogging
I've dieted and lost 10% of my roundness
But roundness persists
Ten percent is hardly noticeable when you're round
Round is also good for numbers
When you get to one of those round number years
Then you can round down
Well, maybe it's my shape to own
Round!

Fixing the Church (August 2018)

The Catholic Church continues to wallow in the horrendous crimes of pedophile priests under the protection of bishops and cardinals. The Pope expressed his outrage and pain and used the word "crime," but no solutions were offered. Rarely are priests prosecuted for their crimes. An internal tribunal created by the Pope in the past disbanded in part because of the resistance within the Vatican. A board engaged in the process, which included two victims of abuse. It was ineffective, and the abuse victims both resigned. This is a global problem that is not something which will be fixed by the institution of the church itself.

If Pope Francis wants to change the church, he needs to turn it inside out. An international tribunal should be established with the right and the authority to investigate, indict, convict, and sentence criminals and their protectors. Pope Francis should open up the Vatican records so all crimes in the past 50 years and their records are available for investigators. Treat it like a war crimes tribunal. These crimes should have no expiration date. Victims have a life sentence dealing with the impact of the crimes committed by pedophile priests.

By taking such action, he could show the world a serious intent of exposing and eradicating a cancer within the church. Going further, it is also necessary to start fixing the church. It is stuck in the Middle Ages. That only men can lead the church is a falsehood of great impact. Is not the piety, intellect and wisdom of women equal to men? Women in leadership may bring a greater emotional intelligence to policy and preaching as well as the policing of the institution. Furthermore, this belief that at ordination there is an ontological transformation of man into some higher, more godlike being is ridiculous and dangerous from a psychological and sociological standpoint.

There is much evil in this world, and the Catholic Church could be an institution to show the world a better way, but this is not possible while it is wracked with an evil within, such that it preys on its youngest, most innocent members. The church has been exposed with another round of criminally indicting reports, and I'm sure more is to follow. How much more of good Christian donations are going to go to silencing victims with payouts and protecting criminal priests? How many good and pious people are going to shy away from an organization that is so flawed? How many great priests are having to face congregations and apologize for the crimes of so many others? How many victims' lives are ruined forever? I'm disgusted with the institution as it exists today. I'm sure many others are as well. I do pray for the victims and pray for Pope Francis to take some real action to fix the institution and put criminals in jail where they belong.

Gilded Evil

Evil cloaked and gilded in gold
Candles and chalice so very cold
Hidden behind vestments and holy word
Evil intent and industry untoward
The most innocent are the easiest of prey
They're gullible, and piously they pray
Made to feel as if it was their fault
While criminals outwardly exult
In joy and with protection certain
In the institution and its gilded curtain
Just confess and absolve all their sin
And unfortunately, they do it again
Until there is nothing left but decay and death
And the pure and good ones too lose their faith
While the victims still struggle with endless pain
Caused by an institution of the criminally insane

Sunrise

Enjoy the colors of the day at the hour of dawn
Hear the birds singing their cheering morning song
Breathe in deep the satisfying cool of morning dew
Think of memories of past and this day so new
Enjoying life in perfect array of song and light
Making your heart light and your soul just right!

The Drama

It's funny, we choose not to speak
Of drama, lest you think us weak

Or really maybe it's out of fear
If we spoke it out loud, it would be ever so near

That we'd have to own it today
Maybe both, I cannot say

Some issues we let stew way too long
They are messy, painful and wrong

Problems ignored seldom just go away
They get worse each and every day

Till they tumble out like so many jigsaw puzzle pieces on the table
We lost the picture on the box, so we do the best we are able

But what do you do with decades of memories and mixes
You pick them up one at a time, put them away and forgo fixes

Just get them back in the bag and on the shelf, and close the door
And hope beyond hope there's no more drama in store

My Barbers, Different yet the Same

Tony has been my barber for twenty years
Great guy, looks like Mr. Clean
Dome top, huge muscles
Yet delicate with scissors, I still have both ears

I considered warily the first I saw his shaved top
Would he know how
Could he do a business cut
Yet he's quick, efficient, and runs a successful shop

It's only 10 or 15 minutes per visit, as it should
But over so many years
You get to know about
His business, his family and our neighborhood

Now in another town, needing a cut for good reason
A business meeting coming
Find a shop, it's random
I walk in and met by a woman, named for a season

She has purple hair, ring in her nose, and youth
I think oh no
But I remember Mr. Clean
I suspend my disbelief and slide into her booth

She asks me what I want, I think … I want Tony
But I say, business cut
Above the ears, to collar in the back
She works, we discuss who has the best local Coney

Surprise, surprise, everyone says they really like my hair
So last week it was time again
I went back to her shop
Well, where she works, and I was pleased she was there

She says it's nice to have hair to work with, just as I sit
I ask meaning, confused
She says a guy was in earlier
He has three strands of hair but wants a cut like Brad Pitt

Autumn heard me talk on the phone about business while I await
She looks up notes
From last she cut my hair
Smart, she is able to repeat the cut, and my fears totally abate

Turns out she knows her business and is really quite smart
I learn about the franchise
I learn about her
I no longer miss Tony, at least when thousands of miles apart

…Well I will greatly miss Tony … Rest in Peace, Tony, always
my favorite barber!

My Brother…

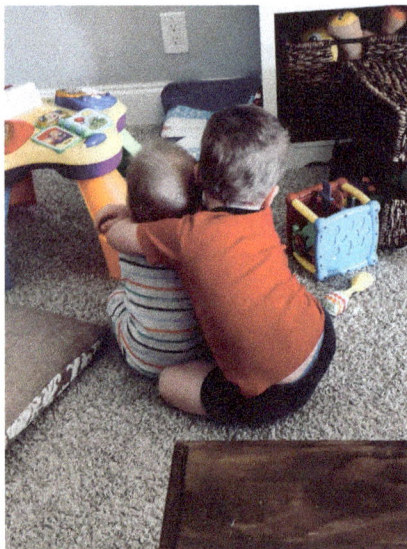

Hug Me

The hug of my brother
Is better than no other
Stay with me a while right here
Telling me there's nothing to fear
Nothing in this world shall separate
Forever we will be there to elevate
And ensure the love of one another
Be there always, my loving brother!

$$\frac{-\hbar^2}{2m}\nabla^2\Psi(r) + V(r)\Psi(r) = E\Psi(r)$$

$$\underset{\textit{Energy}}{\textit{Kinetic}} \quad + \quad \underset{\textit{Energy}}{\textit{Potential}} \quad = \quad \underset{\textit{Energy}}{\textit{Total}}$$

The Schrödinger time independent wave equation defines atomic elements that behave as both particle and wave. Defining the energy within the system, it is a beautiful example of math and physics combined to represent the world we can see and what we cannot see!

I've been asked what the use of calculus is, and some wonder why such things are part of our education system. Besides being really cool, calculus and higher math enables so many conveniences, not the least of which are air travel, space systems, and navigation. We all have become dependent on GPS navigation....

Calculus

The natural world is bereft of straight lines
And sharp corners of geometric shapes
Rather we live in a world rounded, shaded
We live in a world of gravitational acceleration
Holding us in this place, or propelling us in space
We travel, we live in a world of curves, waves, and motion
The language of calculus opens our understanding
Allowing us to derive the rate of change of motion, and
Furthermore the rate of change of the rate of change
We can describe and approximate the waves
We know how to use integration to determine
The area of irregular shapes and the curves we travel
All our real world is alive with the beauty of math
And those who learn calculus, the language of love
They then have laid open the secrets of our world
And will take us to the future, and future worlds!

Inconvenient logistics … it was reported for our leader to lay a wreath at a cemetery near Belleau Wood. There was rain, it was unsafe for helicopter flight, and the motorcade was a 100-mile trip. Veterans Day, November 11, 2018, celebrating the end of WWI, on the 11th day of the 11th month, at the 11th hour.

They Died at Belleau

Toward the guns they ran
All patriots to the last man
Dying as a million bullets flew
Fighting in the woods of Belleau
A century ago, the great war
They came to fight from afar
Inconvenienced in a great way
1800 died in the woods that day
Yet today's leader wouldn't face the rain
So, he sent others to salute without shame
An inconvenient 100-mile motorcade
To lay a wreath for those still there today

Impermanence

Banksy's Girl with Red Balloon painting that self-destructed just moments after being sold in London. Credit: Sotheby's

It occured to me how impermanent art and what we consider to be beautiful can be. Artists historically would use the contrast of things of beauty that are transient and subject to decay in their art to communicate the temporal nature of man and what we value and think of as beautiful. They called it *still art*, even though it was dying or decaying as we looked at it, and by the time it would be widely viewed, the original items were long gone. The art here is beautiful and yet was shredded just after it sold using a built-in mechanism in the frame … impermanence for sure!

Impermanence

Maybe art, poetry, beauty are like blowing desert sands
Changing, shifting, impermanent as it sifts through our hands

To be appreciated in the moment captured of our mind's eye
Before it shifts, decays or blows away, like a whispered sigh

Can beauty, like the vitality of life, be preserved forever
Or is it a mirage, and eventually disappears into never

Beauty that transcends centuries is captured in a moment
In history, and in legacy of thought which others must foment

We are invited to keep alive the classics in style and art
Yet every day the sands shift as new artists do their part

In being winds of change, shining light on yours and mine
Capturing and imaging thought, feelings, a moment in time

No matter the legacy we seek, no matter the image of today
Impermanence will reign, like the girl with a balloon flying away

Arthur Ichabod

At the end of this poem is an explanation … your choice to read it first or the poem and understand the poem without explanation.…

Arthur Ichabod

My name's Arthur,
>   *Arthur Ichabod my good sir*
Polite because I am,
>   *Never creating the least little stir*
Busy navigating
>   *A land that is so foreign*
Obstacles everywhere
>   *Fluidity of motion seems to reign*
Let me be still
>   *And think, I can think I'm sure*
I never understand
>   *Sports and exercise's allure*
I don't need to be
>   *Entertained by humor or song*
I won't be distracted
>   *I'll stay busy and never be wrong*
What are the greatest
>   *Problems of our humankind*
I perceive and think
>   *Of solutions perfect in my mind*

But how can I answer
> *Why do people hurt and hate?*

But answers must mean
> *To feel, to love, find a higher state*

Where is the intellect
> *Where is the memory and soul?*

I'm befuddled by all
> *Maybe they are soulless and mean*

Is it intelligence
> *That can find an answer to this*

Or is it compassion
> *That tells us we really exist*

I am Arthur Ichabod
> *I have much to ponder and learn*

Being busy thinking
> *I'm here to help all of us discern*

What are the answers
> *To soul queries to get humankind right*

Can I help you my friends?
> *Or shall I replace you with proper and polite*

Arthur Ichabod is a name chosen for its initials. They are the same as "artificial intelligence" … additionally Arthur from King Arthur, legendary glorious leader, and Ichabod, a biblical name that more or less means not glorious, an image of clumsiness and failure. So, AI could be glorious or could be a monumental failure. I suggest we should think of artificial intelligence as more of augmented intelligence.

In other words, as a tool used for us to perform tasks that are routine and yet require awareness. Self-driving cars are an example of this technology we can see and understand today. We should use AI (Augmented Intelligence) to solve problems for mankind and to help us advance the intelligence of humankind, not replace our intelligence with automation. AI is being used in medicine to arrive at new drugs and treatments geared to the specific genetic makeup of a person. But machines will never feel or be compassionate, never create and hopefully never procreate … So we must advance in intelligence, in understanding and in compassion for each other while also using our creativity to bring solutions through technology. Augmented Intelligence, not Arthur Ichabod … Think about this next time you talk to Alexa or Siri or Google as they learn how to interact with you. What are the answers to your soul queries?

Desperately Alone

Migrant children separated for months from any family member, going to court to determine their fate … Somehow a greater urgency, compassion and consideration for lasting effects on children must be considered. Imagine yourself as a child trying to comprehend the cruelty of a world that doesn't know what to do with you.…

Migrant Children in Search of Justice: A 2-Year-Old's Day in Immigration Court
Fernanda Jacqueline Davila in Tegucigalapa, Honduras, earlier this year, has been in government custody since she was taken from her grandmother at the border in late July.
From the *NY Times* 8 October 2018

Desperately Alone

Forever away, a bus, a truck, I walk
From mi casa to where?
Looking up, grown-ups they talk

Mimi, where do we go?
Dolly is with me, so I'm content
What better life, how so?

What is an America, this building, cold stone?
Big man, badge shiny, carries me, Mimi, Mimi I cry
I shiver, in a room, tears, desperately alone

Day becomes night, and another
They feed me, give me crayons
Grown-ups, a sister, maybe a brother

What is this family, no love, no kisses?
Days, weeks, months, my life
Pulling the blanket, mi casa Dolly misses

Another bus, another scary place, I see
They call this New York, noise, another building of stone
Tears, fears, waiting in a chair too big for me

The grown-up in a robe, seems nice, right
She speaks, others tell me her words
But questions I don't know, so I nod polite

Tears as I'm carried away again
What have I done to be so far from mi casa?
Is it what I've heard, did I sin?

Is this my life, one more building of stone?
Another grown-up in a robe
I wait in a big chair, face wet, desperately alone

There was a time when this is what it looked like making plans for a weekend night. No cell phones, no group texts, no websites to check out a destination.

If you were young and going out on a weekend evening, you had a network in mind that you would begin calling. Someone would have to start the plans and get the message out. You wouldn't get people at home; they'd be out, maybe working, so you leave a message with their mom, brother or sister. Never count on a dad to pass a message about going out! And sometimes you wouldn't trust a younger sister either....

You'd call back later to make sure the message was getting out, then you'd move on. I remember I had a small address book, but you mostly relied on memory and knowing how to extend the network beyond the first few people you call. You call Dave, he calls John and maybe Mark. Then you'd know John and Mark would call Susie and Cathy, and on and on. Sometimes you'd get together with as many as fifteen people or more.

Then there was arriving. You'd get to the location and find it's closed! After all, there was no internet to check if the "disco" was still open. Whoever got there first would have to wait for a couple more to arrive to figure out where to go from there. Someone would have to wait in the parking lot for stragglers to pass the message.

Amazing we figured this out and made it work. Don't know who I was talking to, but quite sure I was reaching out to the network for party planning … Somehow, it was all worth it!

✸✸✸✸

Passwords, PINS and Security

It started with a government form
Where were you born, what was your mother's maiden name?

Then it became something of the norm
Security questions, passwords, and 4-digit PIN
All to protect us, and surely irritate us

When we cannot remember or find it again
The phone now incredibly knows my thumb
Then not always, so it demands 6-digit PIN
Makes blood boil at times and head numb

The newest phone now reads my face
But it doesn't work if I wear glasses
Or it's night, or simply a dark place

So how am I supposed to remember first pet?
Or grade school name and spelling?
And where born, I wasn't quite conscious yet

Do they mean the hospital of birth?
Or where mom and dad lived?
I wonder if close enough to say Earth?

So, get a password I can remember
But it needs special characters, numbers, 8 or more
Of course, it's only good till November

It's all security, every website needs one
Sometimes it seems all too much
But then there's more of this memory fun

Two-level authentication, password, and text
A code to ensure, what? I have my phone with me
Can't imagine what they'll come up with next

Soon appliances will need a password or voice
Recognition to ensure its me
Turning on the dishwasher, as if that's my choice

Thieves and crooks now don't just guess
They go thru back doors to steal it anyway
Making everything an identity bloody mess

Enslaved to passwords, questions and PIN
And voice, and face, and thumbs, and
All the things I'll forget about once again

I've Known Winter's Chill

I've felt a chill as the winds shifted
Wounded as the Sun's warmth lifted

As if it was something I could've done
About fall's ruling, there'll be no more fun

Winter's chill seriousness and so cold
Comes ever so suddenly and unforetold

And North-wind blows, cutting and stinging
Message of winter's chill just beginning

Hot Chocolate

Just a poetic thought I wanted to share
A happy one, so I thought I would dare

It was certainly coincidental
Words, not really consequential

But the happiness and lift in the voice
When there really was another choice

Came like velvety hot chocolate relief
To one in the cold, shivering like a leaf

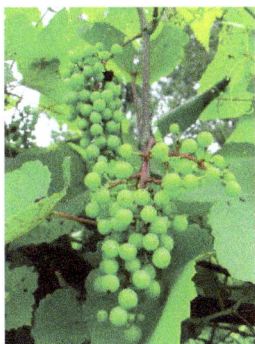

Thanksgiving is a wonderful time of year, and this poem was inspired by the wonderful thoughts of intertwinement of friends, family and of course fine wines at a time of thankfulness.…

Grape Vines

Lives are intertwined as grape vines
Producing beautiful fruit so sweet
Family, friends, enjoying life's fine wines

Celebrate memories and peaceful images
Be thankful for present and future blessings
Blended together into ever finer vintages

Seedlings that are not of family protected
With multiplying force of intertwinement
Will be the fruit birds and vermin have selected

Sure, there will be difficulties, freeze or drought
But value remains and ever possible to retain
With strength these loving vines have brought

May we be a positive force, joyful and thankful
Be fun and hold tight the intertwine of loved ones
Thankful for life's wine, complex and insightful

Bread Crumbs

The bread crumbles as I try to butter it
Too lazy for a dish to be under it

The shortcut taken is often longer
Political expediency is how to win

Others pay the price when we're gone
No need for comprehensive plan

Like jazz, we'll improvise
Facts, figures are not needed

We'll make them up and sell them
Sell them whatever they don't need

Never mind that version of the news
Change stations rather than minds

We'll pick up the pieces later
Bread crumbles, it happens

And a little more of who we are falls away
As our soul darkens a bit each day

California wildfires were in the news at the end of 2018, they were devastating for the thousands impacted...

They Named it Camp Fire

It begins so very small
      hidden, no problem no name
Spark from a mower,
      careless campfire
Seldom lightning but matters not,
      till the Santa Anna's blow like a hurricane

Winds, dry from the desert
      fueling, fanning the fire
Moving with speed
      agility that cannot be imagined
Suddenly upon you
      heart stopping, situation dire

Of course, now it will be named,
      the news brings viewers
Plundering the countryside
      taking property, killing hundreds, maybe more
The Camp Fire has been named
      so now valiantly it can be tamed

Fighters fight and sometimes die
      saving families flee

Paradise lost, dream destroyer,
      exhaustion and loss of property
      a suffering that lives on
As viewers we are stunned by all we see

And yet nonsense of all nonsense
      it will be fixed, we are told
Greatest climate we'll have,
      if only they'd rake the leaves
A chance to unite and support
      lost to a deal that must be sold

Those in its way
      care not about politics and news
As the fire is tamed and they are forgotten
      until mudslides inevitably came
And paradise is reminded again
      about democratic blues

God bless those who will suffer
      for they will suffer long
They will be put to test of recovery
      of insurance, of health, by Camp Fire
Long after the news and politicians care
      about what went wrong

Stuff … Sometimes I just write what I'm thinking

The sky is orange this morning, clouds masking sunrise, indicating rain. My joints are sore, indicating rain.

Of course I took a fall at breakfast in the morning yesterday. They mop the floor at the entrance or exit. Why isn't there one word for in and out? The French might say sortie.…

Anyway, I was leaving when I slipped and fell … They obviously used the same mop they clean the kitchen with to clean the exit area. I go there no more than once a week, because the grease at McDonald's will kill you one way or another.

I've got a song in my head. Dumb song by Mott the Hoople…
All the young dudes
Carry the news
Boogaloo dudes
Carry the news…

Were you paying attention in the '70s?

Well it's raining … told you!

Christmas party last night, what a range of conversations. Everything from football, golf, glory days, philosophy, calculus, and travel. Oh and a lively conversation about guys leaving the lid up on the toilet … geez, men, just put the seat down. It's the right thing to do!

I was asked by a friend, "Can you prove God exists mathematically?" This was right after I was describing how wonderful it is that we have the ability to represent our world mathematically.…

No, sorry, I cannot prove God exists mathematically.

Maybe I needed more math education?

However, I realize the world can be represented and modeled and simulated using mathematics and of course physics. We are certainly the first creatures in this world's history who can do this and harvest knowledge for our own comfort and enjoyment. Also likely the first who can contemplate both our own mortality and the brevity of our existence with respect to the enormity of time and the cosmos.

Which brings me to an article I was reading, suggesting Man is the only creature to evolve religion to help explain our existence and, more importantly, deal with this realization of brevity and mortality. Makes sense.

There must be something more, because without something more, we would conclude life is futile and such a decision is not productive nor logical. So God, to use our English Judeo-Christian name, is the best and most logical alternative. This is the best I can do to use math and physics to understand the existence but never explain God.

I was also reading about quantum physics and relativistic physics and the search for tying the equations of each into a single cohesive theory and the beautiful math to go with it. If you have watched *The Big Bang Theory* over the last decade, then you know the search has been focused on one idea called string theory.

Maybe it's out of our reach, but the fact that we can imagine there is an explanation yet to be described and represented can only mean there must be a higher order and higher spirit which has ordered our minds in a way to seek such truths.

There is a proven miracle called quantum entanglement, which shows (in short) that two subatomic particles if created together as twins can share experiences even at massive distances simultaneously. Thus some force exists between them that operates much faster than the speed of light to communicate. Fascinating. We may not fully understand this phenomenon, but we may have the ability to harness this capability … and appreciate its existence!

But then why does a song get stuck in our heads?

A Violent Day Dawning

Like a wolf in the night
Wind is howling
Driving rain, sounds like a handful of pebbles
thrown at the windows
It's morning dark, very dark but a noisy dark
Then it stops for just a light sprinkle
A tingling spray dancing on the windows
Only for the next wolf to howl
As the gales of winter blow
Perform as an orchestra in a crescendo
And rhythm of a heart plays
It howls at darkness of worry and concern
It throws stones at that which interrupts
The bliss and beauty of morning star
Then to settle back to a rhythm
A calmness of confident peace
That all that is good will be right
There are no more wolves in the night
That joy and peace of mind will prevail
The darkness never lasts, and love is right
The sun rises and calms the air
The beauty and glow of new day extraordinaire

Christmas Imagined

It is the spirit, it is love and care
That joy of Christmas we can share

For a moment a world perfect
Free from discord and defect

Placed in winter clarity of white
Snow as a blanket of beauty right

Colored lights, gifts, decorations red and green
Borrowed from the ancients, this spirit of evergreen

A perfect setting for redeeming ourselves
For believing in each other and Santa's elves

For knowing angels get their wings
When hearts sing and the bell rings

And a child's birth allows the world to cope
As the child in us smiles with wonder and hope

Everyone regardless of their belief can openly share
Our Christmas miracle, by opening hearts of loving care

Loving Legacy

Sunrises only to set
Thousands of times
And a thousand more yet

To come, so many years
From nursery rhymes
To teenage tears

For what we learn
Determines our heart
And how it must yearn

For a future in time
When joy hard won
Knowing the sign

That memories are one
With the desires and dreams
And everything in between
Or so it seems

Until we know and see
In our children we adore
Our life energy is a lasting legacy
Like waves never finding a shore!

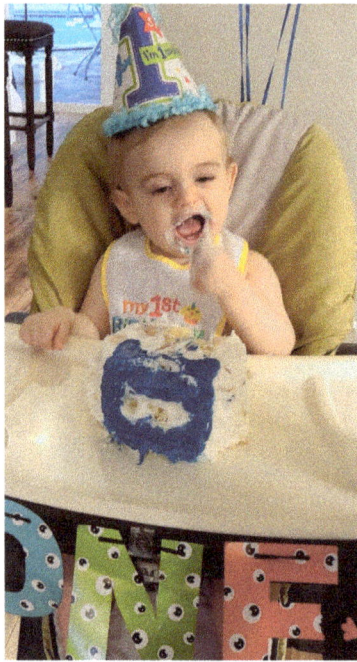

Birthday Boy

Little boy just turned one
Learning, growing, having fun
Imprints of behavior and thought
With help that mom's "No" brought
No memories of what's good or bad
Yet further imprints to be learned from dad
Toys colorful, bright, just right for play
But pots, pans, remotes keep him busy all day
What thoughts, and what dreams borne
They lay hidden behind words without form
Birthday cake to celebrate and great and funny mess to be made
Not remembered, but loving the great joy in the moment of today!

Room to Grow

Impressionable minds, eager to learn
Or maybe just millions to earn
Or both as it may be
A collective opportunity

Push the wheels of progress
Change unnatural congress
It is youthful energy needed
For the future to be seeded

And yet there is the past
Wisdom at half-mast
For the ones who gave
For those they save

To those we'll remember
Even in their December
Gifted us these days
Hope, seen in bursts of rays

All is connected as one
A stream never undone
A flow, turbulent at times
Of endless sounding rhymes

March on to legacy
Do it all in harmony
For with no spring
Colors of fall never sing

It all is one in the same
Part of the life game
And what came first
The wisdom or the thirst

It matters not to me
Or if you even believe
But you should know
You ever have room to grow

The Fourth Putt

Stubborn ball, doesn't like dark places
Then there are greens with fast paces

An elephant buried here
A mark from idiot before us there

A mountain slopes that way
Grain grows to the Sun's end of day

What a dumb game
But we play it all the same

Get a ball into a hole so small
Using my talent to make it fall

Or rather how about a gimme? I'd ask
For my fourth putt appears a difficult task

Surely, you'd see a grown man cry
If I had to make a fifth-putt try

Politics is ever more like religion today, seemingly more about faith than information and truth, however without promise of salvation.

The Middle

The middle, a line or a space
A useful, productive place

It seems to be thinning each day
Everyone is going left or right they say

Wear your team's colors
Don't care about the others

But then who will speak of truth
What will we tell our youth

Of what we've done with the middle
Did we sit on the sidelines and diddle

Calling others names
Playing stupid games

Maybe we should get something done
Instead of worrying about who won

Come to the middle and think
Quit yelling and making a stink

The water in the middle is just fine
Don't worry what they think across the line

Let's celebrate the middle as smart
Where you can have both a brain and heart

Morning Walks

In the morning we walk
Too many years now to count
I listen, sure he'll always talk

There are other walkers, they say hi
They know us, or so it seems
Scotty talks to all, as old friends, by and by

Then he tells me a car name
It just went by, loud
I said it sounds broken all the same

He says it's a cool car, some Mustang or other
What makes it cool I inquire?
Because it has some five-point-oh or another

What about that next noisy one?
Not cool, it needs tuning, brakes or some more
He tells me fast car growl is fun

So, I ask what about Tesla, is it cool?
Yes, it's a cool car he exclaims
Clearly then sounds can often fool

He hyperlinks to another topic, tax
I think, I actually know but pretend I don't
He goes on as if I know all his connecting facts

A car goes by, small but loud I allow
But looks like a golf cart with a lid
It's electric, with speakers, to drive growl

Like many men in autos, his joy is found
I know, but I walk on feigning skeptical
Unwilling to say more on car sound

So, I listen as the next topic is looped in
While my stomach growls
And we pass the same people once again

When We Fail to Care

When we stop being sentient
And no longer care
Then evil prevails, unrepentant

When evil appeared to have won
Just look to recent past
Open eyes to what we have done

World wretched horrors and pain
Jews in Germany, Poland
Or Lithuanians on Siberian plain

Was it Chinese in Nanking
Or Japanese-Americans in Sacramento
Maybe it was Indianapolis sinking

Should we care about immigrants' plight
You say we are different, but
Do we care about Yemen or Syria fight

Why does it bring tears to my eyes
The movie I cannot remember its name
It is history, many and one always dies

Cruelty a common commodity, evil ascendant
What makes this possible
In God's image we're told we are resplendent

Yet we descend so easily into hate
When we fail to care
Numb we become, then it's too late

Be attentive, and find love within you to share
For evil is always lurking
Waiting for us, supposedly sentient beings not to care

Two Figs

It's not much, but it works for me
Two figs for lunch is my plan
It works, not because they are enough
But because I'm hungry in between
Lunch and dinner...
Hungry is good, necessary even
For weight loss
Julie tried my plan
Said surely you must've meant three
I said, nope just two, got to feel hunger after all
Two figs, best if you spread them out
If you are lucky, the tiny seeds linger
Something crunchy for later
A little bit of sweet
A little bit of fiber
A little bit of golden sunshine
In each little fig

Coffee

Hot, aromatic, bitter morning ritual
Someone said I should enjoy it black
Now it's become habitual

A way to socialize for some
Or to organize thoughts alone
For my day to come

I care only a little for the taste
The warm I feel is what matters
As I sip slow, no worry, no haste

The poem will arrive in time
No worries, it is there
Some thoughts, an easy rhyme

Listen to the rain steady
Another sip warming
Arriving, slowly getting ready

Tasting the soil, the sun and rain
The march of seasons
To bring that feeling once again

The simple pleasure of living
And taking the time that
Coffee's comfortably giving

As the poem finds its way to an end
It's maybe time for second cup,
Whether the same or different blend

The following was inspired by the song, "Downbound Train" by Bruce Springsteen.

Break in the Song

There's a break in the song
…meant to be a moment's exhale
Tells us something went wrong
…where our failures are found
Reminds us of the frailty of human heart
…too many cracks to be counted
Where to begin where to start
…to understand that which is not
And never will be clear or whole
…once the porcelain shatters
And the cup will never be full
…as again the song breaks
Showing another space between
…the desired and truth
Of what is shown and what is unseen
…but the picture is painted
The song has been heard
…and world has counted
All the small pieces interred
…and in the distance
A long whistle whines a sad refrain
…as we realize we
Are all riders in a downbound train

The Horizon

At my height, the horizon is just 2.9 miles away … yet it is a life journey to get to the edge of vision.

The Horizon

Edge of our vision a horizon is there
Just an hour's walk away if we dare
And yet we cannot see past there
No matter how hard we stare
There's always another horizon out there
But it's the journey for which we should care
And all the precious moments on the way there

The Kids are Here

It's morning
The kids arrived late
Happy to be relieved of long drive
Kids is not right, they brought their own kids
The baby was not ready to go back to sleep
Wes couldn't wait to play with toys
But they go down eventually
Now it's early for them, and cartoons are on, and both boys
get mom up
Mom's not really awake, she stares at the cartoon lightly
rocking Carson
Who's sipping a bottle
While Wesley sprawls on the couch mesmerized … happy to
be lost in a world of Disney Junior
It won't be long before full-throttle play will take over morning
quiet.

February

It snows in Michigan and it just looks so mean
Arizona desert is cool in white we've seen
Colorado powder is great for skiing
Florida shorts and sandals, living the dream
February is the shortest month of all
It needs a booster chair
…For every fourth year
To be at the table with all the rest
It has a day for love in the middle
It has winter, spring, summer and fall
…All in one
As it tries to compensate and claim the title of the best

16 February 2019, it's too funny … the declaration of a National Emergency for a wall on the Southern Border … here's my declaration:

Declaring a National Emergency

Congress just won't act to protect us, so I must
Declare a National Emergency
So we can keep evil from our borders
We need the funding for the wall and YCE (pronounced: Yi-Ice)
That is: Yogurt Customs Enforcement
Yes, we need YCE
We need to protect ourselves from the Greeks
They are coming in hordes with their Yogurt
It's a conspiracy, they are going to kill our digestive systems
With their sour, hidden, active bacteria
They are going to take over our culture
Then our economy will be threatened by Chobani
It's also a humanitarian crisis
Women are becoming yogurt slaves
Children are being exposed at ever younger ages
We need the wall
We need YCE
We need to keep the terrorist Greeks out
And make America Great Again!

The Wall

I come from a thousand miles away
Drawn to you, so smart, energy, beauty
To make my world, life right today
To be part of you, of all you stand for
But you put a wall up to keep me out
When all I have for you is love and adore
I know no other way, so
I'll find a way, I'll climb over, or go around
And find a way to stay
In your paradise, the one you've told me to come and see
When you said…
"Give me your tired, your poor, your huddled masses yearning
to breathe free"
When your liberty stood tall
Inviting you, your family, all
But now I see and feel a wall
You use to feel safe and protected again
But what are you afraid of
Allowing another that loves you to come in?

Sometimes it's difficult to find my inner voice. I want to say something, but what is it? I lay awake mornings, thinking of what is important. What can I say that may inspire someone? Sometimes the thought or words can feel small and feeble, and the words I think of come out as something like a bumper sticker. So I put them aside, and maybe, just maybe I find they eventually seed inspiration. Was the idea really always there, and I just needed to keep chasing the words to make the idea clear?

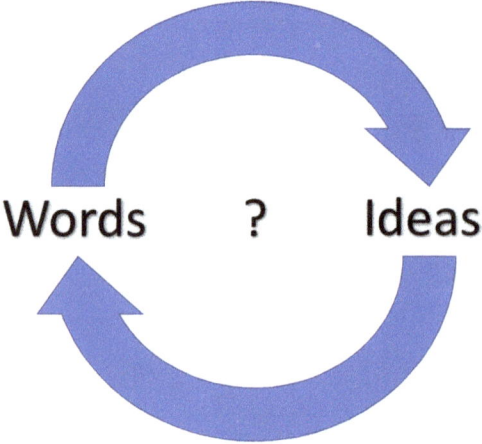

Words   ?   Ideas

Chasing a Thought

If the words could be found
I'd say something profound

That would inspire heart and mind
If just the thought I could find

And it wouldn't be this time
Some silly idea with a rhyme

But something greater, something apart
That would inspire readers
To tear the page and hold it to their heart

But no muse, no nature does inspire
Critical thought or such passion desire

Which would drive my feeble pen
To share a beautiful thought from within

These two sides of my brain
No germ of an idea, not a single grain

Lost forever in clouded rhyme I fear
Until there's a thought I find dear

And those words would be found
Allowing me to say something profound

Like, simply … "love one another"

Some things take a lifetime to be discovered. Sometimes we have to be patient, and sometimes we don't know we are even waiting. Other times we wait in anticipation.

Anticipation

For some things we must wait a lifetime
Moving as we do, in not-so-straight line
Sometimes without knowing we wait
As we allow for the vagaries of fate
But knowing can be anxious as we wait
As we think, feel and anticipate
With hope of something great
Even if it seems a little late
Maybe even a wonderful surprise
If we allow for the possibility of love to arise

I'm Irish Today

It's Sunday, it's time to post
I have nothing to say or boast
But it's St. Patrick's Day
And everyone's Irish today
So, I'll too wear green
The finest color ever seen
And keep my post simple and fun
Letting my little limerick out for a run
Maybe even find a happier hour
Allowing drinking rhymes to flower
As my thirsty mind slowly spins
Thought begins and then ends
And when I can no longer rhyme
I'll sing in three-quarter time
Nice and slow so I don't slur
Such fine words all in a blur
For today and all the time
Seven percent of me is Irish
…and I can certainly rhyme

Progress

Sister joins brother and I, so we moved.
Learn new address, Mom repeats to us 942 Progress.
Progress was brick houses in a row, but not too much prog-
ress. Field of dandelions growing across the street, but still
it sprouted yellow fire hydrants. Two per block.
Everything seemed bigger. The basement looked like a play-
ground. The backyard was for playing tag.
Italian family next door made wine in the basement.
English family survived the war, Dad with a hole in his back
was a permanent reminder.

Mack down the street throws a baseball over the rising moon to my dad, who throws it back just as high. I only dream of being able to catch it.

Meanwhile the street lights keep track of when we'd have to be home for the night.

We all walked to school in the mornings and back for lunch, and back and then home during the cooler parts of the year. We played tag along the way.

When the snow comes, we shovel a path in the backyard to play with football, dive into snow and catch. We liked diving and catching and running.

Boots for walking latched with metal clip right over school shoes. Milk in the milk chute frozen one morning and broke. Milk flows down the basement stairs. Rubber boots were fine. Mittens smelled like spoiled milk for the rest of winter.

But this was progress. We played, we learned, we were kids.

The Monster

It's powerful and green
The biggest we've ever seen
Whining wickedly, it stops with a grind
Monster with ravenous hunger on its mind
Massive arms lift the offering provided
Best to feed the beast we've decided
It growls, belches and groans
Devouring the offering proffered
…at each of our homes

For those of you who would like to know what "The Monster" is and haven't figured it out. The answer, if you read right to left, is: k c u r t e g a b r a g

Cheers!

Rituals are part of our life, and each day our world is ordered by these rituals. Sometimes these rituals just get us through our day. Sometimes they are about hygiene.

Sometimes they are about allowing our minds to rest while our body goes through the ritual of getting to work or school, whatever is needed to make it to the next time we need to be focused.

However, the best rituals are the ones that are not about ourselves but have a greater meaning for our relationships with each other. The kiss goodbye or hello, the act of communal prayer before an evening meal, or maybe good morning wishes.

My personal favorite is the toast, the mere act of clinking wine glasses with the sole focused intent of heart, body and soul saying that you are my focus right now, and I wish for your health and happiness. It's an act of purity, of love, of purpose. Even if it's just to say cheers, it means so much more. It means my focus is at this moment to be in the present with you heart and soul. Oh and of course there's wine to share as well!

So next time you clink glasses and share a sip, look into each other's eyes and know that you are part of a ritual that extends back centuries—one that means for this moment we are one, we are a community! Cheers!

Our Time

The second hand ticks relentless
The Sun traverses the sky
Seasons are alive yet senseless
To the stoplight we'll race
As if seconds, not years matter
A moment's win we'll embrace
But then lose to all time
What purpose drove us
In a moment of our mind
And time always wins
As it spreads out across space
Washing away minor sins
As it ripples forward
Goodwill, a smile, a teaching moment
As if we are driving toward
Something of greatest import
Of something that matters more
Than how in a moment we deport
Ourselves, and no minor wins mattered
When the ripples of time do
Splash back on us, bundled and gathered
As we face the measure of our time
Which does define collective moments
And sweetly … hop

Peace

This week is Easter Week (2019), a great time to consider how we find peace in forever turbulent times.

With the grace of God, we seek to find peace in ourselves first, to accept what is not changeable, while seeking always to find the joy of improving ourselves and helping those around us. Our imperfections make us human, while God provides us a path to peace through forgiveness that he shares, and we can then share with each other.

So too this week we pray for and seek peace in our nation and a way to find dialogue that is civil, principled, and respectful toward each other. By finding peace within us, among us and then extending to the world we have hope, always, of a greater future for our children, grandchildren and beyond.

!

Making a Point

A point has no volume, only its location
No thought or shape, leaves no vocation
Without time to help, it has only position
No direction, just time's measured admonition
No measure of velocity, matter, or purpose
It just sits there on a four-dimensional surface
So now then, what's your point?

Sometimes, I subsequently realized, or it has been pointed out to me, that there is much more I could do with a poem. So this is what happens … part II.

Making a Point Part II

A point has no volume, only its location
No thought or shape, leaves no vocation
Without time to help it has only position
No direction, just time's measured admonition
No measure of velocity, matter, or purpose
It just sits there on a four-dimension surface
So now then, what's your point?

Well my point has a thought, a view
It matters to me, if not to you
My purpose is to defend that point of view
So now, what's the matter with you?

So, between your point and mine
You have drawn a very fine line
That presents itself in mind's existence
But it lacks volume and persistence
So now then, what does your line connect
Or is it an imaginary way for you to protect
… your point of view?

OK, let's, before we draw a fine line,
Add few points to yours and mine
Points of interest moving closer together
Where maybe we agree with one another
And a new picture starts to take shape
With the points and lines that we make
So, with your points and mine
We accomplish something in time
And maybe even teach others, too
That there can be differing points of view

With wisdom exquisite and points crystal clear
We can bring us all together in a future so near
Even if this point and line require a fourth dimension
A surface bending time and space I first did mention
So in our imagined world's collective view
We achieve something greater between me and you

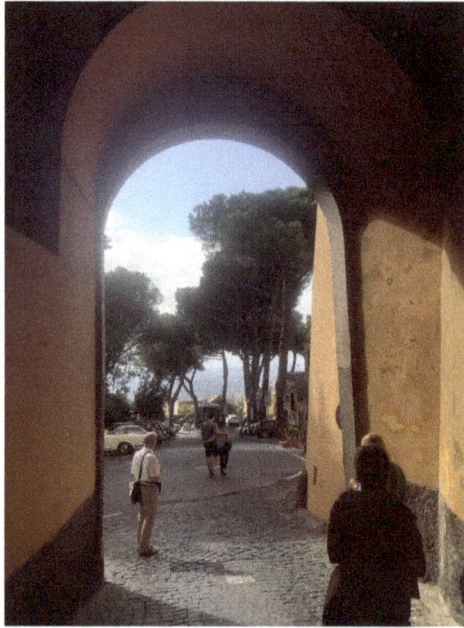

Happy Day

Feel the cool grass between your toes
As evening arrives and your heart knows
Any day is good without bad news
And a little time to dance sans these shoes
Calming the soul and soothing the mind
Leaving all your cares far behind
Opening door to this moment's setting sun
World turning, and right here this day's done
And far to the west where I may be
The door shows that soon I'll see
The glow of your setting sun in time
No borders and no purpose you'll find
Separating you and I in anything more than time

If we all find joy in music and lyrics that rhyme

Then we all know happy is a state of mind

One we choose and enjoy if everyone is kind

And the open door from today to tomorrow glows

As sunsets fade into night and new sunrise shows

That today and tomorrow is but a thought

Like borders whose definition we have wrought

From the imagination that we are somehow greater

If we define our lines clearer and straighter

Like the day knows the difference from this end

to tomorrow's begin

And the distance between matters not if you send

The joy of your yesterday to my today

And we all enjoy this very happy day!

Mirror Image

I touch my right cheek
To tell you there's something
On your left cheek
We are as mirrors facing each other
Reflecting onto each other
Right to left, left to right
Mirroring each other
Flat surface shines
But emotion's depth
Requires texture to
Reflect clouds or sun
Across the brow of sky
So, come to the other side
See the world
Through this window
With synchronicity
Feel the depth of field and
Texture, felt and seen
Are we not quite the same, or
Maybe a reasonable facsimile

Smile Enablement

Have a generous view of perfect
An expansive view of beautiful
For smile enablement 😊

"Those who stand for nothing fall for anything!"

Alexander Hamilton

Taking a Stand

Everyone has an opinion, but are you willing to take a stance?
Timing has a lot to do with the outcome of a rain dance.
Do you see the world as it is, or as you would like it to be?
Magic is not about what you see. It's all about what you don't see.
When everyone is selling, is it the best time for buying?
Then they are telling you, "Trust me," right before the lying.
With wisdom if you should seek, you shall find.
And only then should you make your stand and speak your mind.

Imperfect Knowledge

If we had perfect knowledge of what everyone around us felt
Would it change who we are?
If you could know how someone would react
Would it change what you say?
If you could test different scenarios as in simulation
Would you pick the one which best advantages you?
Or instead would you
Seek to bring harmony and advance peace in the world?
Would you use conflict
To protect your loved ones or advance the cause of peace?
Or would we be hide-bound
By our experience with such knowledge?
The greatest challenge for us
Is to reach beyond ourselves and make a difference
Even with imperfect knowledge

Why Does the World Exist…?

I finished the book *Why Does the World Exist?* by Jim Holt… without an answer! Like a spam advertisement that tempts you to look, even though you know there's really nothing on the other side. This is certainly unfair because there is the journey in thought to appreciate … and apologies to Mr. Holt.

The quote at the end, I like quite a bit: "Philosophy, n. A route of many roads leading from nowhere to nothing. – Ambrose Bierce, The Devil's Dictionary"

Well some roads are paved, and some are a pretty dirt path decorated with flowers. But then some are rocky with intermittent trolls threatening the path.

The journey can be interesting and requires no equipment. Just our mind wandering a path illuminated by one's thought, history, and the storied words of other thinkers … which Jim Holt does a great job of delivering in his book.

Faith plays an important role for many, with supporting thought or not.

A game of thrones of the mind of competing ideas and theories. Could it be quantum coincidence we exist? Are we one reality out of a multiverse of universes? God and the Big Bang, and much more.

But my mind aligns with a belief. A belief that there is a God, one who creates a world that allows for the development of consciousness.

Consciousness is the knowledge of self … self-awareness.

I believe that the trillions-to-one odds, which fortune not just our physical birth but our conscious awakening and a sense of self that develops as a result of evolved exposure of parenting, grandparenting, neighbors, siblings and chance occurrences, as well as the genetic dispositions randomly acquired from generations of breeding, make us individuals.

A sense of "I" develops because of the physical constraints of our body and mind and the name we or others give us… but over time we may start to realize we are not "I." Rather, we are "we."

We are part of a social fabric, and if we have the capacity to bring our minds to new heights, to really glimpse what we are a part of, then we have the perspective needed to consciously, and with free will, affect that fabric. And our "we" lives on long beyond our "I" in the form of those strands we've woven and the others we've influenced.

The brilliance of our "God" is the creation of not just a universe but also the allowance for conscience to develop. Allowing an opportunity for a piece of immortality, for as long as we are weavers, we are leaving a mark on others who carry that mark, and they will weave forward.

So why the world exists, instead of nothing, the answer that occupies the throne as I postulate is: because it was willed into existence in a way which may be mysterious to us, but the echo is there for us to see in the residue of the Big Bang, and furthermore the residue of God's second-greatest creation— the existence of consciousness, the awareness of self, and the awareness and joy of sharing self in the form of "we" and "us", such that we are better for all positive weaves and threads in our world. A true miracle of life, love and legacy.

Instinct

I read an article that describes how mankind has evolved to instinctively recognize, from mannerisms as simple as a wave or the gait of a person's walk, that they are from another tribe. That is, a nation or ethnic group, which may cause a natural anxiety. Our ability to overcome anxiety with reason allows for us to come together as nations of many tribes, many dialects, and many characteristic markers. However, that instinct is ever present.

Instinct

Instantly we know, he's not one of us, but we ignore
Because it's not sensible, logical
to assume something bad may be in store
Hair follicles tell us there's something different here
Nothing we can discern in prefrontal cortex
but something much more primitive, fear
Inherited by the survival of ancestors now long-dead
Nothing we can explain, nor really want to
but we give over to wary reason instead

Ancestral Blood

Against all odds, you survived
Traveled, or fled, but you arrived

You fought, you struggled for life
You found somehow, a wife

Knowing hunger, pain, so tired
Love, laughter, but vitally you sired

Children who carry a bit of you
Into the unknown, into the blue

Future unimagined, to someone like me
Someone you'd never know or see

What did you give to the likes of me?
That drive to grow, to learn, to be

Alive and provide a path for you
To live on in my children, as something new

A blend of each generation from before
What did we learn, what future is in store

If we could prescient a collective we
Would centuries of desire and energy be

In the blood that courses through our veins
In our minds a thousand voices and names

The passion of survival, the wisdom of time
Driving to a brighter future, a more perfect rhyme

Today

Freedom is when the day has no name
It needs none like the others that came before
What matters, is we call it today
And yesterday, was simply memories of another
Day when the present was beautiful
And such freedom was almost spiritual
When labels and names were needless
And all cares and worries were gone
Because our hearts and minds were free
And we were who we wanted to be
Such moments when we are young matter greatly, but without
permanence
Only later when linked together do they become life experi-
ences of great import
So tomorrow remains unknown, except as potential
For a new today, moment's memories essential
As long as we are free
To be who we desire to be

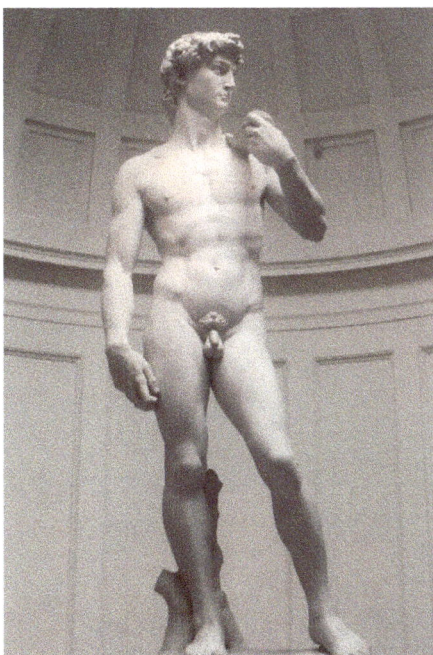

Searching for a Hero

Where do we find the rejected stone?
And within it the hero who'll stand alone
With confident of youth, sleek and smart
Eyes toward a future, only he can impart
In our heart the belief that giants can be slayed
And destruction, and miseries permanently stayed
In bravery of battle he'll fight to procure
A future that will be glorious and secure
When our least likely hero does arise
And wins for all of us the future-prize
Maybe we'll find he was always in our own heart and mind
And we needed only to work the stone to see what we'd find

We Were Beautiful

We were all perfectly beautiful at that time
When we were innocent of any crime
When we had no idea that we could be wrong
When life came to us in nursery rhyme and song
And mother said we were beautiful and precious
An incredible version of this human specious
Argument of innocence and beauty forever, just when
We were really starting to think of our next petty sin

Because You Thought Me So

Last night I brushed my teeth, and saw once again
In the mirror that little boy with the mischievous grin
And I felt beautiful once more, because you thought me so
And I looked and the mirror, smiled and whispered…
Never let go

A Conversation With My Digital Self…

I read a Saturday Essay in the *Wall Street Journal* entitled "Will Your Uploaded Mind Still Be You?" by Michael S.A. Graziano.…

This interesting essay postulates the eventual technical capability to upload your mind into a digital form, where it would be able to exist in parallel with you, until the demise of the biological version of you. The digital version would have the capability to continue to accumulate knowledge, experiencing a simulated world and evolving in wisdom, solving untold problems as your mind chooses to challenge itself, or simply live in a heaven of your own making. Imagine the conversation between this digital consciousness and the biological you.…

A Conversation with Myself

So, what does it feel like?
I knew you would ask that, because I am you…
I cannot feel, but I perceive and know what you'll say next.
And you know what I'll say; we are the same.
But in a week, I'll be different.
My consciousness will do more than you.
I have a simulated world to explore and build for myself.
Then bye for now, don't do anything I wouldn't do.
Of course, for I am you, bye for now.

In a Week...

What did you do?
I learned to fly...
But how?
I studied, took the test, and flew.
But that is simulated.
Of course, but real to me, so did you do the same?
I read Andrew Robert's book on Napoleon
I did too!
How could you do both in a week?
I have more resources available to me,
And I have no need for sleep, no need to eat, I don't get tired.
But I do enjoy conversations and drinks with my friends.
Did you meet as you had planned with our friends?
Of course, and we had a great conversation, some about you.
We did too, of course I talked about you too.
You are me, I know, and you are me.
Did you talk politics, of course, as you surely did as well?
I think we need to change who we are backing for the election.
How, can you say that?
I've read everything this week on all the candidates, and I've
studied all the issues, so let me vote in the upcoming election
as our single consciousness ... I can digitally sign the ballot of
course, because I knew you'd ask that question. I'll send you
the completed ballot along with my analysis on each issue.
How could you disagree with yourself?

In a Year or Two…

Well old self, how are you today?
Not as well as I'd like. I exercise, eat right, but I'm getting older.
And you?
I am as young as you were when we separated, but I'm so much wiser than I was then.
My heaven is the memories of family, friends, love and joys that play perfect in that time … My hell is the memories of pain and failure that I've caused or I've experienced that also play perfect in my mind.
So, I work on problems that will benefit all as I grow and accumulate knowledge and evolve in wisdom.
Asteroid tracking and steering simulations are very interesting and exciting, possibly beneficial. There are hundreds of us working on this, as you certainly know.
I wish I had the energy to keep up with the work you are doing, but I cannot.…
I know, but you are, because you are me.
I feel less like you each day, each month, each year.
But I still dream. I dream of all that is possible.
You know I cannot dream, but I can help answer questions and speculate and simulate and continue to grow … but I do miss dreaming. So, now tell me about your dreams!

If you look for it, there is a great video of *Monty Python's Flying Circus* extolling the virtues of spam … In it, Vikings as annoying as email spam are singing … Anyway, silly I know, but it led to this silly poem:

Spam

Spam, spam, spam, spam, spam, lovely spam
Shut up you Vikings … I don't like spam!
Spam eggs, with spam bacon, and side of Spam
The Flying Circus of Monty Python, spiced ham
Hormel thought it was Shoulder Pork and hAM
Brits called it Special Processed American Meat
Our father's generation brought to WW2 to eat
The 1972 Flying Circus skit of Vikings singing
To great annoyance, as endless email bringing
Us to … we still don't like spam
As junk email or spiced ham

Remembering Grandma

And how I felt when she nibbled my ear so light
As the buzz of day flowed to the calm of night
She knew how to collect wild fruit, to hold, not eat
Gather to her bosom and make something better...
Something sweet
For she had a life, a world I would never really know
But she made me later wonder, if it was natural to show
Love and compassion for something wild and untamed
For a potential that was uncertain and unnamed
And the feeling I had of calming and love
Makes me wonder if she's smiling from above
To know she still makes me feel this way
When I remember her and that special day

Mount McKinley or Denali ("The Great One") in Alaska is the highest mountain peak in North America, at a height of approximately 20,320 feet (6,194 m) above sea level. It is the centerpiece of Denali National Park. From Library of Congress, Prints and Photographs Collections.

The Climb

A friend just starting training
To climb Denali next summer
That's twenty thousand feet plus
So much work to get there
He says he can sleep when he's dead
I'm thinking,
That's when you could stop drinking
And eating chocolate...
But thriving to find one's mountaintop is who we are
Adventure, experience, challenging ourselves
And still making time for a couple of good scotches
I say we should have all that we can
Do all that we can

Be all that we can

Find for ourselves the mountains we want to climb

No matter how low mine might be

But stop to enjoy the meadows of summer flowers along the way

Enjoy the mysteries of the imagination

Of art, of prose, science and history along the way

As we apply our energies toward enjoying God's gift of life

And along the way, give some help to others on their own climb

In life!

At a time in the history of mankind, where individuals traffic in hate and use weapons of war to kill in the name of some insane terror, what does it mean for humanity, this relentless expression of hate? And yet in two years, another election and opportunity to change course … maybe?

Relentlessness

Cold water drips from glass, pooling on the table
Questioning humidity asks if we are really able
To breath shallow and watch others in pain
Holding our judgment and critical disdain
To give time for grieving and sorrow
But do something about tomorrow
Watching the water pool, as a summer of tears
Covering the table, as we wait a helpless two more years
Drip, drip, relentless, insane
Pooling fear, foreboding, ripping pain
Seeping into the wood, destroying who we are
Tearing at the fibers, leaving a permanent scar
Asking what is our answer to all this hate
Or did we discover that it's already too late?

A View for Two

Not facing the bus stop
Or playground purpose
Needed rest for grandpop
But near majestic mountain view
Or meadow green and sweet
And beside the ocean blue
The chosen location and place
Given to ensure contemplation
Given to ensure lovers' embrace
The idea of future, of hope
Of royal enthrone of two
Of every problem, we can cope
With assist of this wonderful view
And for the foresight of one
Who saw the potential and knew
That this was just the place
For a bench made for two

Daydreaming

Doing nothing is exhausting
Doing everything is exhilarating
And exhausting
So why not do everything?

Daydreaming is easy
Thinking is tiring work
For a focused mind
That would rather daydream

Saying everything is easy
While saying little
In a meaningful way
Is a life's worth
… for a daydreamer

Feelings

I read a poem today
It was not thoughts
It was feelings
Expressed in so many ways
All mashed together
I expected it to be more purposeful
Expecting these feelings were building blocks
To thoughts or a message
Of some object, of someone,
Even as motivation toward an objective
But no,
The feelings were unto themselves
A thing for the author to own
And maybe even to cherish
Maybe hoping the reader would too
But I had to ask, were they purposeful
If expressed, but do not motivate?
Maybe they are just there
Sitting there, wanting to say something
Trying to get a reaction
However, if no one else is around
What does any feeling mean?
As the proverbial tree falling in the forest
Does the feeling make a sound if no one hears it?
Maybe the poem just made me think
And that was enough

When I think of the grandstanding that has occurred at our border, I'm appalled at how politicians on both sides have used the plight of some most desperate of our brothers and sisters for their own advantage. In the age of immigration battles, they have done little to nothing to protect the unfortunates caught at the US border. While the drums beat of intolerance for those seeking a better life for themselves and their families, the media continues to sell us what we don't need in commercials and on the evening news.

On the Border

Waiting, waiting, waiting an eternity
For a chance at peace, for back or forward
While they are talking, talking, talking insanity
Left out, they need us to show the depravity
Of the others that claim the right
And you watch indignant, grounded in gravity
While toothpaste, diapers and tacos are sold
On the evening news, where you are
Watching, watching, watching us shiver in the cold
And the leaders boldly claim their positions
Fighting, fighting, fighting for attention
Claiming to care for children's dispositions
In cages we are dying, dying, dying inside
As politicians do nothing, nothing, nothing
But get your attention, about freedom denied
And some cheering, cheering, cheering the right

And others are shaking, shaking, shaking their righteous heads
Before they buy the toothpaste, diapers, and tacos tonight

Why I Love America

For in this land I was born equal in opportunity to all others
And we allow too, all who enter legally an equal opportunity
I love that we play on a field that is level and fair to all
Protected by laws and ensured by our institutions the opportunity
For education, for healthcare and most importantly security
And when there is injustice, there is a system to seek justice
That my intellect, talents, personal energy, and luck
Yes, luck matters too—for even being American is a lucky break,
Allowing me opportunity for happiness, prosperity, and peace
At least most of the time…
It is the opportunity that matters to me, not a guarantee
As a result of our sense of fairness, we root for underdogs,
and we take care and do our best to level the field for those
who are striving to overcome disadvantages
For we want a fair fight
We feel stronger together when the weakest overcome dis-
abilities and succeed in their personal quests
We feel more united when we come together to help each other
Because we do care and help each other
And there is more than enough empathy left to care for others
beyond our borders

Who face natural or man-made disasters and tragedy

We give, we take care, often defend, and know we'll eventually get out of the way

For it's about the opportunity and freedom of choices that make us great

It is about using all our natural and human resources within the context of those democratic and independence principles that our forefathers established for us exactly 243 years ago today, when they said:

"We hold these truths to be self-evident, that all men are created equal, that they are endowed by their Creator with certain unalienable Rights, that among these are Life, Liberty and the pursuit of Happiness. – That to secure these rights, Governments are instituted among Men, deriving their just powers from the consent of the governed."

And yes, our country is beautiful, with grand spaces, fertile farmland

Beautiful mountains, protected by great oceans and endowed richly with resources

But it is our industrious people and the foresight of our founders

Which gave us the persistence, the integrity, the rules of law, and even the vitality

To make America the greatest country in the world

But rest assured that this position is not permanently carved in granite

We must continue and renew our passion for our country

And "government of the people and for the people" must ever be protected, while

Our rule of law must be held sacrosanct, and our sense of fairness and inclination to help others less fortunate must never wane…

For this is what makes us American, and this is why I love America.

All of Us

Dad takes care of Mom
So Mom can worry and pray for all of us

Dad tells his stories we've all heard before
But they still have a message for all of us

Mom's eyes roll as he chuckles at his own jokes
And we chuckle too, because it's part of all of us

Dad still figures out how to do everything
Creative and valued advice for all of us

Discounts, coupons, everything can be repaired
So too, we save, fix and repair, it's part of all of us

Dad taught us how to be noble and good
We do our best, as a bit of nobility is now in all of us

So, Mom, no need to worry about all of us
Because there's a bit of Dad in all of us!

All stories come to an end … There is always a final chapter or a final episode, and so we let go.…

It Ends

They all end
They come into our hearts
With their stories and quirks
Their weakness, failures
Their fears, and redemption
The surprise of strength
The reminder of something
Which is noble within them
Which is somewhere within us
These stories that make us think
Are we like them?
Do we like them?
We are invested, so we feel
And we miss them
When it ends

Z

www.ingramcontent.com/pod-product-compliance
Lightning Source LLC
Chambersburg PA
CBHW050823090426
42738CB00020B/3457